RIGHTEOUS SAUL
V.
RIGHTEOUS PAUL

Paul White

Righteous Saul v. Righteous Paul
By Paul White
Copyright © 2018 by Paul White

Published by Paul White Ministries
P.O. Box 1030 ▪ Flowery Branch, GA 30542
www.paulwhiteministries.com ▪ United States of America
The author can be contacted at info@paulwhiteministries.com ▪ 661.294.5078

Cover design by Barry Sempsrott

Book preparation by Shannon Crowley, Treasure Image & Publishing
TreasureImagePublishing.com ▪ 248.403.8046

CONTENTS

ACKNOWLEDGEMENTS

Special thanks to Shannon Crowley for her time and expertise in bringing this book into existence. It began with a conversation, and from there, she transcribed, assembled, and ultimately sent the work to print. Along the way, she endured my additions, rewrites and many questions. She remains a consummate professional.

Thanks go out, as well, to Barry Sempsrott for his masterful work on the cover design. He has made countless flyers for our meetings over the years, and now may his latest creation aid in leading someone into liberty. I know that is his life's aim.

INTRODUCTION

Every life needs meaning. Meaning gives definition to the things that matter to us, and when life meets us with chaos and confusion, what sustains us will be our commitment to the things that matter. What matters to me are those whom God has given to me, which are my family and those closest to my heart.

I'm sure you feel the same. We each take our love for what matters and channel it into our meaning for living. My meaning is wrapped up in the call and the gift to present the good news of Christ and His finished work. My family matters to me, thus my meaning is wrapped up in them, and I want them to dwell in the best possible version of the world.

I believe an understanding of the good news of God's love and grace will provide for that world, and thus, I find myself passionate, to release God's children into the knowledge of the liberty that He has paid for.

As sons and daughters of God, I believe that we *matter* to the heart of our Father. When He wrapped Himself in flesh and became a man, Jesus gave *meaning* to what matters. When life met Him with chaos and confusion, we mattered so much to Him, that moving forward became His meaning.

His desire to create for us a better world, on the other side of the cross, with an empty tomb and limitless possibilities, moved Him forward through His own Passion. Love and grace have provided the liberty we so desperately needed, and we are now, finally, coming to realize that it is ours, free of charge.

NO LONGER SLAVES

In this hour, I believe the Father has called me to be an evangelist to the evangelized, teaching believers about who they are in Christ. Decades of church experience, has convinced me that many of us are functioning day-to-day with the mentality of a servant rather than the identity of a son. We're constantly working for God, hoping to be "used" by Him. At the end of the day we hope, pray, and cross our fingers that we've done enough to please God. Our day could have been so much richer and fuller if we had only lived as sons and daughters—having received what He's done for us.

Sonship, as a doctrine, is often attacked on the premise that such a message will produce a lazy Church. I would agree with that premise if it were merely a doctrine. However, the concept of sons and daughters is more than a doctrine; it is the key to proper identity in Christ.

It is within the context of relationship, that display when father is home, the children feel free while the servants feel nervous. A liberated people, full of identity, will create a free church, and a free people will always produce more than a people in bondage!

There will be more production that comes out of a house full of sons and daughters than could ever come from a house full of servants.

John 11:44
And he who had died came out bound hand and foot with graveclothes, and his face was

wrapped with a cloth. Jesus said to them, "Loose him, and let him go."

In the ministry entrusted to me, I take serious the previous injunction of Jesus. When He raised Lazarus from the dead, He looked to His disciples, and to those closest to Lazarus to, "Loose him and let him go." Jesus did not remove the grave clothes off of resurrected people, but He has entrusted that job to us.

He has finished the work in giving resurrection life (a job we can never do) to all those who believe. Our role is to release our brothers and our sisters from the guilt, shame and condemnation that emanates from this world, from the enemy, and from religion.

In reality, we are often releasing the same people whom we have previously helped to bind! These characteristics manifest as grave clothes that cover people, trapping them and making movement impossible. Their hands of creativity are stifled by failed performance; their feet of mobility held motionless by fear; their ears unable to hear due to a misled desire to work for their favor; their eyes covered from seeing truth due to the blindfold of their own failures. The list goes on and on.

This could be part of what Jesus meant when He breathed on His disciples and said, *"Receive the Holy Spirit ... Whosever sins you remit, they are remitted. Whosever sins you retain are retained"* (John 20:22–23). Jesus wasn't giving His disciples the ability to wash away sins, but rather He was giving them the ability to help people to retain, or to be released from, the condemnation that comes with sin.

Every time we open our mouths, we have the awesome power to bind or release someone. You have the power to slap them with guilt, shame and condemnation. You have the power to make them feel as if they haven't lived up to certain demands, or worked hard enough for their favor, or done enough to please God, (as if they're not slaving hard enough for the Father).

Equally, you have the power to present the love of the Father, manifested through the cross. You have the power to set hearts at ease with the truth that grace is enough and that the blood works on their behalf. You have the power to give people an identity as part of God's family through faith in Christ.

Condemnation is easy to achieve by simply stacking someone's works against someone else's works, and there is always going to be someone doing more for you to compete with. Someone will have always read more than you, prayed more, fasted more, gave more, did more, or went more. Someone will always beat us if we are looking at a list of righteousnesses and works. In that environment, we will always have a slave mentality, and we will always come up short.

When, and if, we finally come to the knowledge of sonship, our experience with the Father will cease to be defined by a passion–driven, purpose–driven and destiny–driven life, and will shift to the presence–drawn life. While always sustained by our commitment to the things that matter, they won't push us forward as much as remind us of who we are and *why* we are. We will move forward as we are drawn into the presence of the one who loved us and gave Himself for us.

In the church, we've been so driven, that in many cases, there is nothing left but the ashes of what was once a burning bush. My family and I spent a few years living in California, where brush fires were quite common. No one was ever excited to see a brush fire— they represented consumption and created a world of chaos. Moses did not turn inside to see a brush fire in the wilderness—they are too common to bother with— but he did turn aside to see a bush burn that was not consumed (Exodus 3:3). That is a sight to see!

I think it's about time that the church burn with a fire that does not consume and leave ashes in its wake. When this happens there will be a light that goes forth from the family of God in which people see no trail of tears. No more dust and broken bones. No more working for God till there's no joy left; no happiness left; no comfort left and finally, no life left.

Your life, your joy, and your meaning should never be sacrificed at the altar of ministry or that of the church. You have the opportunity to love life and see good days (1 Peter 3:10).

We do not dwell in an Old Covenant world of performances, full of a list of "do's and don'ts," where good advice abounds. Instead, we dwell in a New Covenant world of "It is finished," where there is good news, that the work has been finished on our behalf.

RECOVERING THE LOST

I think the Bible is less a story of people coming out of sin into salvation and more a story of lost sons coming home.

> *Luke 19:9-10*
> *And Jesus said to him, "Today salvation has come to this house, because he also is a son of Abraham; for the Son of Man has come to seek and to save that which was lost."*

Jesus didn't say, "I have come to seek and to save the sinner." While He does save sinners—and thank God for that—it is not what Jesus said He come to do. When He said, "I have come to seek and to save that which was lost," it's easy to think He is referring to sinners, for sinners are surely lost, but that isn't the definition of "lost" that Jesus seemed to be going for.

14

<u>*Matthew 15:24*</u>

But He answered and said, "I was not sent except to the lost sheep of the house of Israel."

When Jesus said, "I come to seek and save that which was lost," He was referring to the lost house of Israel. The house of Israel consisted of the sons of Abraham. We might refer to them as the family—the ones in God's favor, His hand, and His will. He came to seek and to save that which was already His, but had lost its way. Consider the irrational action of leaving the ninety-nine sheep behind, to go and find the one that was lost (Luke 15:4–7).

I realize Jesus did not call it irrational, but wouldn't you? I would! Nobody abandons ninety-nine sheep to go find one that is lost. They wouldn't leave the multitude to search for one—they would just count it lost. It's logical, and economical. But God's love and grace for us is neither logical, nor economical, and it certainly is not rational. We surely aren't worth searching for, and yet, our Good Shepherd left the ninety-nine to find us. We are that important to the heart of God. He loves us that much!

It's irrational for someone to spend money to throw a party to celebrate money they have found. Yet, Jesus tells the story of a woman who turned her house upside down to find her most precious coin. When she found it, she called her friends together and threw a party to spend that coin (Luke 15:8–10). Does spending money to celebrate the fact that you found a coin seem irrational? Welcome to grace: an irrational love of God! It's irrational that He would love you so much, to celebrate to this extent, because He has found that which was lost.

I think this is the message the church needs in this hour. We are a flock of scattered, lost sheep that need to know the irrational love of our Shepherd. Or, worse still, we have scattered and lost sons and daughters who need to know the love of their Father, which is where the "irrational grace" of Luke 15 goes next.

The third story in the "Lost" trilogy of Luke 15 is the story we often refer to as the "Prodigal Son," but it is really the story of a father. As in the previous two (1 of 99; woman with lost coin), this story is a celebration of the return of things lost, be it a sheep, a coin, or a prodigal son.

<u>*Luke 15:11-12*</u>
Then He said: "A certain man had two sons. And the younger of them said to his father, 'Father, give me the portion of goods that falls to me.' So he divided to them his livelihood.

The father distributed the inheritance to his two sons. The younger spent it all and ended up slopping hogs in a foreign land in order to survive. The older son took his inheritance, and went out to his father's fields to work.

The younger son finally tired of his lifestyle and what it had done to him, so he determined to go home and offer himself to his father as a hired hand. When he arrived at the end of the lane, his father ran to meet him, gave him shoes, a robe and a ring, and killed a calf for a feast. The father refused to hear the boy's speech about being a servant.

During this ecstatic reunion, the older brother was out in the fields, laboring away—breaking his back for an inheritance that was already his. This son was serving his father, whom perhaps he didn't view as a father (maybe he sees him as more of a taskmaster?).

When the father entreated him to come and join the feast, to celebrate the return of the younger brother, the older son responded bitterly, "See how much have I done for you, and you've never killed the fatted calf for me" (v. 28–30).

The father answered with a statement we all need to take to heart. When we read the story of "the prodigal son," we usually think of our drug-addicted cousin or our neighbor in prison—those out slopping hogs who need to "get saved." However, we fail to realize that we may have someone in the pew next to us that is perhaps the older son—out in the field working for the approval of a father he doesn't know loves him. The tragedy is that he had never comprehended what the father meant when he said to him, *"Son! All that I ever had is yours"* (Luke 15:31).

The story of the prodigal son ends in tragedy, as the older son doesn't realize, that everything belonged to him. All he had to do was appropriate it through the covenant of a father and son, and receive it as his own. It would be another tragedy for me to write a book about righteousness and not inform you that all that the Father has for you is absolutely yours and you can appropriate it by faith. All you need to do is walk into Daddy's house and receive it.

FREEDOM AND SONSHIP

I believe the message of sonship is frightening to some because they fear that people will take advantage of being a son and do some things they may have avoided before. Perhaps we fear that if people were to hear that they are sons, they would stop working so hard. If we release them from performance, what if they just run off?

I liken that to a dog chained in the backyard, which is there only for the enjoyment of his owner. Surely he wouldn't choose that yard if it meant remaining on the chain. Of course, the dog is chained because he is uncontrollable and his owner doesn't want him to run away and wreak havoc in the neighborhood.

I can't help but wonder why the owner wants a dog that doesn't want to live in his yard? The illustration may be silly, and I'm quite sure I'm missing the point of the dog–owner dynamic, but I think the concept is similar to what we are doing (or are having done to us) by religion. We are chained so that we can stay "under control," or maybe we are chained because we have been taught that to leave the "yard" is to leave the Lord.

The true love challenge might be to release the dog from the chain and let him run (though your neighbor and animal control may have something to say about that). If that dog loves his master and his home, he knows where his food and water bowl are, and he knows how to come home.

This is what we must do with people in the church: release them into the glorious liberty of sonship by removing the grave clothes that have chained them and kept them in the yard. The Holy Spirit is alive in our hearts and He leads us home to the Father—to a place where we feed in Him and where we find rest for our souls.

So again, the Bible is certainly a story of sinners becoming saints, but maybe more so of sons coming into sonship, and lost sheep coming back into the fold—people who are religious; full of performance; full of works; coming into a revelatory knowledge that the Father loves them without their performance and their works.

One of the greatest revelations I ever received came when I was on the brink of spiritual burnout, and had nearly had enough with ministry, and with the church at large. I was raised in a pastor's home, and a life fully integrated with ministry was all I had ever known. I knew religion and the associated lifestyle of pushing the church millstone—grinding the corn so the church can grow, grow, grow—over, and over, and over again. Before long, I was exhausted with religious performance.

Once sonship was revealed to me, a whole new world opened. I saw value in just knowing God and being known by Him. The process of going from being performance-minded, to identity-minded took a lot of un-training, retooling, and a bit of detoxing off the drug of my own performance. The process was necessary if I were to come into the knowledge of who I am as a child of God. The glory of the redeemed—the right to call ourselves the sons of God (John 1:12) is ours by inheritance, but settling into that mentality is a journey. It may start on a Sunday morning, and then it rolls over into our lives—into our work week, into our relationships—as we are released into the liberty of who He has created us to be.

In this little book, we take a look at the ultimate example of religious performance and the story of one man's most radical transformation. We will track with Saul of the New Testament (not Old Testament Saul … that guy is an entirely different problem!), through the machinery of works and achievement, to the depths of hell, where zeal finds it starkest expression.

In Saul we will find a member of the family—the ultimate lost sheep. In his encounter with Jesus, we will see our own selves, grappling with who we are and yearning to break forth into who we are meant to be. We will watch Saul transform to Paul—not merely as a public profession that a change has occurred, but as the end result of a confrontation with the Light of the world.

Like Saul, blinded on the road to Damascus, we must each confront our own religious zeal in the face of our Lord Jesus, and then confront our blindness as well. Saul entered the encounter with his eyes wide open to his own ability and self-righteousness, only to have them darkened to those realities. When the scales fell from his eyes (Acts 9:18), he walked out of the home of Ananias and began a journey into sonship. Saul went in, but Paul came out.

If you head into this book confident in your ability to live for God, do the right thing, curry favor through your perseverance, or if you are exhausted from trying, then I pray that you too become blinded to your own ability so that your eyes can be opened to His love and finished work on your behalf. Go into this journey as a Saul—that's fine—but come out the other side, a Paul.

Chapter One

WHO IS SAUL?

Perhaps our greatest example of a lost, wandering son returning home, is the Apostle Paul. When we consider him before his conversion, we often think of the terrorist who persecuted Christians, dragging men and women to prison (Acts 8:3) and breathing out threats of murder against Christ's followers (Acts 9:1–19).

In that version, it is easy to picture him as a wild-eyed demon on a first-century religious purge. However, that picture of him has probably been filtered through our understanding of what we think of a sinner, acting in cold blood, rather than of a religious zealot, acting by sanction of a governing body. In any case, what we think of Saul and what Saul thought of himself are stories of contrast.

Acts 13:9

> *Then Saul, who also is called Paul, filled with*
> *the Holy Spirit, looked intently at him ...*

INTRODUCING SAUL

Prior to Acts 13, we know Paul only as Saul. Saul had Jewish pedigree and a distinguished background. Not only a highly educated and intelligent man, he was one of a slim minority of people in the world of that day who could read and write

Saul could trace his lineage back to Abraham. By all accounts, he knew all there was to know about Jewish culture, faith, and religion. His attack against the early church (known as the Way) came less from a place of hatred toward Jesus, and more from a place of devotion and zeal for the God of Abraham, Isaac and Jacob.

For Saul, those Jewish adherents to the Way (and all the adherents were Jewish at this point) were a threat to pure Judaism. If one were to receive the man named Jesus as the Messiah that was one thing, because the definition of Messiah could be argued.

Does Messiah overthrow Rome? Can Messiah be killed? Declaring Jesus to be "the one" is perhaps not enough to get one in trouble with the authorities. However, it was another thing entirely to declare that Jesus was the Son of God—that His death was simply a prelude to His Resurrection, and that He lives in the hearts of those who believe on Him and are baptized into the faith. That was a step too far for Saul to tolerate.

The hierarchy of Israel had seen to it that Jesus was crucified by the Romans (as opposed to being stoned by the Jews), making his death on wood evidence of his blasphemy (Deuteronomy 21:23), and any religious adherent knows that you don't hitch your star to someone who is cursed of God.

Saul simply could not allow this perceived poison to remain in the midst of his Judaism. A little leaven would leaven the whole lump, and Saul must have considered it his righteous obligation as a zealous Jew to remove that leaven so that the God of his fathers could be vindicated and His holiness upheld.

Let's not confuse Saul with anything less than a passionate zealot. Don't think of him as less concerned with holiness or strict adherence to Torah. In many ways, everything Saul did and represented would have been viewed with respect and honor by both the religious and secular world of his day. One could not accuse him of failing to live up to the strictest standards of Jewish holiness, nor could he be accused of being unfaithful to the traditions of his forefathers.

He was loyal in his synagogue attendance, consistent in his public readings from the Scriptures, and was, no doubt, a paragon of excellence in regards to the keeping of dietary, sanitary, and moral laws. No one could accuse Saul of Tarsus of doing anything less than his very best in the eyes of God, and good Jewish folk would probably have agreed that in regards to the life of Saul, "God must be well-pleased."

ON THE WAY TO DAMASCUS

Acts 9:1-2
Then Saul, still breathing threats and murder against the disciples of the Lord, went to the high

priest and asked letters from him to the synagogues of Damascus, so that if he found any who were of the Way, whether men or women, he might bring them bound to Jerusalem.

We first find Saul on his way to persecute members of the Way, complete with written authorization to imprison those who follow Jesus of Nazareth. This journey was perhaps a bit tame compared to some of his previous encounters with the disciples of Christ. Remember, it was Saul who stood by in silent approval as the raging mob killed Stephen the Evangelist.

Acts 7:57-59

Then they cried out with a loud voice, stopped their ears, and ran at him with one accord; and they cast him out of the city and stoned him. And the witnesses laid down their clothes at the feet of a young man named Saul. And they stoned Stephen ...

Saul attacked with ferocity and fervor, thinking he was doing God a favor. Jesus had told His disciples that this would be the case, only adding to their persuasion

that they were right in having chosen to follow Him
(John 16:2).

> *Acts 9:3-5*
>
> As he journeyed he came near Damascus,
> and suddenly a light shone around him from
> heaven. Then he fell to the ground, and heard a
> voice saying to him, "Saul, Saul, why are you
> persecuting Me?"
>
> And he said, "Who are You, Lord?"
>
> Then the Lord said, "I am Jesus, whom you
> are persecuting. It is hard for you to kick against
> the goads."

Saul had a direct encounter with Jesus—the very
One he was persecuting. Consider that last statement in
light of the fact that there is no verse that shows Saul
persecuting the man, Jesus—but that's not the point.
Attack the Father's kids, and you are attacking the
Father!

The revelation on the road to Damascus did not
come at the end of a week of fasting and seeking God.
Saul was not being rewarded for his faithfulness and

perseverance. His moment was not the culmination of activities that have proven his worth—it was an anomaly. Saul had an encounter he did not deserve nor that he had earned. Jesus found him in the middle of his terrorism and revealed Himself to him.

Perhaps it shows that if Saul can be reached in the middle of his issues, anyone can be reached in their own!

GOODBYE SAUL

<u>Acts 13:2, 6-12</u>

As they ministered to the Lord and fasted, the Holy Spirit said, "Now separate to Me Barnabas and Saul for the work to which I have called them ..."

Now when they had gone through the island to Paphos, they found a certain sorcerer, a false prophet, a Jew whose name was Bar–Jesus, who was with the proconsul, Sergius Paulus, an intelligent man. This man called for Barnabas and Saul and sought to hear the word of God.

But Elymas the sorcerer (for so his name is translated) withstood them, seeking to turn the proconsul away from the faith. Then Saul, who also is called Paul, filled with the Holy Spirit, looked intently at him and said, "O full of all deceit and all fraud, you son of the devil, you enemy of all righteousness, will you not cease perverting the straight ways of the Lord? And now, indeed, the hand of the Lord is upon you, and you shall be blind, not seeing the sun for a time."

And immediately a dark mist fell on him, and he went around seeking someone to lead him by the hand. Then the proconsul believed, when he saw what had been done, being astonished at the teaching of the Lord.

In the middle of Acts 13 there is a change, and the book shifts from the character of Saul to that of Paul, and never returns to the former again.

This is an interesting moment in the biblical narrative. Saul takes on the name of Paul in the same passage in which he prays that another man lose his sight, just as Saul had lost his own on the Damascus road.

The author could be connecting the reader to that event, and showing that Paul had learned his lesson. He was no longer like Saul, obsessed with his own righteousness. Now, he is Paul the humble, living out the gospel for Elymas the sorcerer in the same manner the gospel worked for him. Elymas is a witch who is intent on turning people away from the faith—namely the proconsul Sergius Paulus. When the proconsul sees the miracle of Elymas being made blind, it serves to open his own eyes to the truth. Saul could not have missed the irony.

To Be Made Blind

Paul's miracle of taking away a man's sight bothered me for a long time. If he had made a blind man to see, I could understand that; Jesus did that sort of thing all the time. In fact, it was one of the things Jesus claimed He was anointed to do (Luke 4:18). But we don't see Jesus giving someone leprosy, or making a healthy man into a lame one. His ministry was the opposite of such darkness. In the story of the healing of the man born blind, Jesus claims, *"As long as I am in the world, I am the light of the world"* (John 9:5).

But a deeper examination into that very story, the one in which Jesus spit on the ground and made clay with which to anoint the blind man's eyes before sending him to his healing bath at the pool of Siloam, shows an interesting postscript to the miracle.

After the Pharisees excommunicated the man from the temple (more on those rascals later), Jesus found him and introduced Himself as the Son of God. Then comes this fascinating passage:

> *John 9:39*
> And Jesus said, "For judgment I have come into this world, that those who do not see may see, and that those who see may be made blind."

First of all, the word *"for"* is from the Greek, *eis*, which is most commonly translated *"into,"* and I believe that lines up with the theme of Jesus' ministry in John. In the previous chapter, he claims to judge no one (8:15). Three chapters after the story of the blind man, He declares the time of judgment to be, "now," and that if He is lifted up from the earth, He would draw all of it into Himself (12:31–32).

So rather than Jesus declaring that He is here to judge, it appears He is telling the man that He is here, *to be judged.* His judgment is not to make blind men see and vice versa, but He is entering into a judgment, the end result of which will be that blind men can see, and those who think they can see will be blinded.

Can we be sure? Look at his immediate confrontation with the Pharisees after he tells the man about judgment:

<u>John 9:40-41</u>
> *Then some of the Pharisees who were with Him heard these words, and said to Him, "Are we blind also?"*
>
> *Jesus said to them, "If you were blind, you would have no sin; but now you say, 'We see.' Therefore your sin remains."*

There's the key! *"If you were blind, you would have no sin."* It would seem that Jesus is telling the Pharisees that the purpose of Him entering into judgment is to open man's eyes to a reality he hasn't seen, and to close them to a reality he is accustomed to.

If they were blinded in the right manner, it would open up a world of sinlessness to them. Adam and Eve had their eyes opened to their nakedness in the Garden and then functioned from shame and condemnation. That shame led to the ultimate cover-up, where they fashioned an apron of fig leaves, created a separation, and hid from God. Their eyes were indeed opened, but not to the glory of their Creator. All they could see was their own performance, and man spiraled out of control.

Christ came to make blind men see, but in a far greater way than mere human eyesight. His death on the cross was to blind men to their shame and guilt, freeing them from condemnation, so that He could open their eyes to a whole new creation. The Pharisees' claim that they were not blind was evidence that they were—at least in the spiritual sense that Jesus was referencing. They were blind to true righteousness, and the fact that they couldn't see the Jesus that was right in front of them was enough to show they couldn't see at all.

When Saul met that same Jesus on the road to Damascus, the end result was heart transformation and the physical act of having his eyes blinded (Acts 9:8–9). It would seem that the object lesson started by Jesus in John 9, continues into Acts 9 with Saul. By blinding Saul to who he was, He can open Paul's eyes to who he could be.

When the Spirit came upon him, "immediately" the scales fell from his eyes and he received his sight, "at once" (Acts 9:18). These two phrases, "immediately," and "at once," seem redundant, but it could indicate how important this lesson is for both Saul and the reader. When the Spirit does His work, He changes your field of vision from a life revolving around you and your effort to one focused on Christ and who He is in you.

This helps with the awkward moment of Elymas being made blind so that Sergius Paulus could be made to "see," in a spiritual sense. Paul is living out the statement of Jesus. The man who thinks he has insight is blinded, while another man who is spiritually blind has his eyes opened to the truth.

We don't know the end result for Elymas, but it seems that, based upon Paul's own history with having his eyes darkened and opened, he is hoping for a similar outcome for this man. This affliction was temporary; not a permanent curse. When the fog lifted, let's hope Elymas had his eyes opened in more ways than one.

In the immediacy of one moment, Saul was transformed into a new creation. Now, in a similar moment, he takes on a new name to accompany his new identity. His two-step transformation is a microcosm of our walk with Christ. We meet Him in faith and are changed into His image from glory to glory. It doesn't all occur overnight—as identity sometimes takes a while to develop—but the de-construction / re-construction process moves us from one place to another. For Saul, the story unfolds quickly, but for us it may take a while longer. Either way, it is worth the journey.

In the moment that Paul surfaces in the book of Acts, we can't know for sure what revelations pop up inside of him. But we can know that future revelations—revelations that will change the church and the course of human history—are planted in that moment. Revelations like those found in Galatians 3 and 4 were birthed in Paul. He transitioned into the knowledge that he had led his life as if he were a mere servant—just like a child unable to come into his own inheritance.

Chapter Two

THE LAW, ZEAL, AND RIGHTEOUSNESS

My background is religion. Some people had the vice of drugs, alcohol or violence, but my vice became my performance and my religion. It is pretty hard to overcome your own performance—you get drunk on your own ability to do good, and you chase success every time you fail. You become intoxicated with your own ability to perform for God, until you think that your ability and performance is what defines you.

In Philippians 3, Paul utilized the powerful testimony he had in comparing the new Paul experience against his old Saul experience. The latter is a bit of an insight into the way I viewed my own self in my religious background, and I suspect it's the same for many others.

Let's take a look at what Paul says about himself and about the church at Philippi.

> *Philippians 3:3-6*
>
> *For we are the circumcision, who worship God in the Spirit, rejoice in Christ Jesus, and have no confidence in the flesh, though I also might have confidence in the flesh.*
>
> *If anyone else thinks he may have confidence in the flesh, I more so: circumcised the eighth day, of the stock of Israel, of the tribe of Benjamin, a Hebrew of the Hebrews; concerning the law, a Pharisee; concerning zeal, persecuting the church; concerning the righteousness which is in the law, blameless.*

The third verse opens with a rather controversial statement: "We are the circumcision ... (who) rejoice in Christ Jesus." He treads on the identity of his own heritage by failing to say, "We are the circumcision ... who are of Abraham." That would have been technically correct in his Jewish theology.

However, he identifies true circumcision as an internal identity in Christ rather than an external identity in Abraham. To claim to "be" the circumcision because you have accepted Christ is path–breaking knowledge. It sets Paul on the path of either fresh revelation or rank heresy. For some, the jury is still out.

Paul further claims that those in Christ, "Have no confidence in the flesh." Let's not rush past this phrase, for it is the underpinning to Paul's argument. Confidence in the flesh refers to the literal circumcision that gave Judaism its confidence. The cutting of the foreskin connected the man to his past, unified him with his neighbor in the present, and set them all apart for the future. Paul used the phrase with double meaning in Philippians 3:4. This is what it looked like (parenthesis mine):

> *Philippians 3:4-6*
> *... and have no confidence in the flesh* **(circumcision),** *though I also might have confidence in the flesh* **(my works).**
>
> *If anyone else thinks he may have confidence in the flesh, I more so: circumcised the eighth day, of the stock of Israel, of the tribe of Benjamin, a Hebrew of the Hebrews; concerning*

*the law, a Pharisee; concerning zeal, persecuting
the church; concerning the righteousness which is
in the law, blameless.*

In addition to listing a few of the reasons that Paul
(Saul) had for being confident in his flesh (family history;
pedigree; education), he proceeds to lay out the
framework for a three-point lesson on the performance-
righteousness standards of someone who is taking their
confidence in the flesh.

- Concerning the law
- Concerning zeal
- Concerning righteousness

Concerning the law, he both understood and kept it
to the level of a Pharisee. Concerning zeal, he was
zealous to the point of overseeing the execution of
Stephen and pursuing the arrest and conviction of
those who claimed Christ to be Messiah. Concerning
righteousness, he considered himself blameless (a
heady claim to say the least!).

In short, concerning the three things he considered most important in his Judaism, he gave them his full effort, and was confident that his effort stacked up favorably against anyone.

Imagine that you could meet pre-Damascus road Saul. His assessment of his own ability leads one to predict that he may go to lengths to determine what "works" you were performing so that he could do you one better.

Perhaps he would discover how often you did something and he would strive to do it one more time than you. "How often do you fast? Then, I'll fast one day longer. How much do you give? I'll give 1% more. How often do you go to the temple? I'll go an extra day—because I'm blameless concerning the law, concerning zeal, and concerning righteousness."

Each of Paul's final assessments—concerning the law, zeal, righteousness—make up the framework of a performance-based mindset that is still alive and well in the church today.

They can be better interpreted this way:

1. What I Do
2. How I Do It
3. What To Expect Because of What I Do

Most of us have been inundated with this tri–fold philosophy for so long that we have mistaken it with authentic Christianity, failing to realize that its proponent was the Saul of a pre–Jesus experience rather than the Paul of a revelation of grace.

Concerning the Law (What I Do)

"Concerning the law, I was a Pharisee." This is what he did—what he did was the law—and he was so good at it that he would have been called a Pharisee.

Our understanding of Pharisees is greatly influenced and—probably entirely shaped by—the role they played during the earthly ministry of Jesus. This is handy in that it works for the duality of good and evil. On one side is good Jesus, and on the other, sneaky Pharisees. However cozy this understanding may be, it fails to get to the heart of the matter in regards to both who the

Pharisees were and how they were viewed by society at large.

The Jew in the first century did not align himself with certain sects the way many do in today's culture. Now we have Reformed and Conservative and Orthodox and others. That isn't to say that divisions did not exist, for they did, but they existed at the top of the food chain, where the hierarchical structure was top heavy with groups such as the Sadducees and the Pharisees. The man on the street was living to survive—highly religious by today's standards—but far less concerned with street debate and piety than we might believe.

The Pharisees were guardians of oral law and tradition. They felt that in addition to Torah, there were rabbinical teachings that should be held on par with those of Moses.

These additions are sometimes characterized as "traditions of men," in the arguments of Jesus. We look back on the other side of the cross and shake our head at their additions and traditions. But the people of that world, in that day, would have seen a Pharisee as the complete package spiritually: someone who knew the Scriptures and the traditions and strove to live them to their fullest.

A Pharisee was less a power-player; they left that to the heady Sadducees, who were in charge of caring for the temple, and in most cases, providing the office of High Priest. Doctrinally, the two were separated by at least a couple of major points: the Pharisees believed in an after-life while the Sadducees did not, and the Pharisees tendency to oral tradition irked the Sadducees to no end. For them, it was "Torah or bust."

Socially, the difference was rather stark. Pharisees were a hodgepodge of talent, education and financial status. Their place at the top of the food chain was almost entirely due to effort and piety. They weren't in charge of the glorious temple, and they didn't have the family lineage of priesthood. Pharisees were self-made men. We have evidence that they came from all walks of life and all financial classes. Some were highly educated scribes, who hand copied the ancient texts, while others were common merchants and farmers.

We toss about the phrase "Pharisaical" to describe someone who is self-righteous or hypocritical, and Jesus called them as much. But don't confuse our understanding of that word with theirs, in that day. To be Pharisaical would have been a high compliment. It meant you had worked hard at your holiness, risen above the masses, and earned what few men had the time or the inclination to strive for. If you were a Pharisee, not only did you think you were better than others, those others thought you were better than them too!

So concerning the law, Paul chose the greatest picture of keeping the law with which to identify himself: a Pharisee. Paul had a right to brag about keeping the externals of the law. These represent what Paul did in the name of righteousness.

CONCERNING THE ZEAL (HOW I DO IT)

Philippians 3:6a
    Concerning zeal, persecuting the church …

Zeal is energy, excitement, emotion, dedication, drive, passion, or fire. There is probably no more promoted thought or ideology in the world today than that of attacking each task with energy, drive, or dedication. The church is not immune, and in fact, has embraced the concept of zeal with, well, zeal. We put on high-energy services with exciting music that appeals to various emotions. We promote dedication to the Lord, the family, and the local church. We build that church with a passion for the lost, a drive to win our community, and a "fire for God." Zeal and its various iterations are never in short supply.

Of course none of the preceding are wrong. They simply are what they are. One could possibly even argue that a church, a family, or a world completely void of these descriptions would be too dull to survive. However, the balance and focus of these seem vital to the good health of the object.

Consider the zeal of Saul. Insert all of the definitions of zeal into his actions. They fit like a glove. Where did this lead him? By his own admission, and the account of the Book of Acts, it led him to persecute the church, and ultimately, the Lord Jesus. How could something so pure and wonderful as zeal end in such tragedy?

Note that Paul is *defining and defending* each of the three positions central to his Judaism: law, zeal, and righteousness. He is putting zeal on par with the law and righteousness—an interesting comparison to say the least. Perhaps in Saul's world, things weren't much different than they are in our own. Not only did the rules have to be followed in order to make one righteous, but one should have "passion" and "drive" and "excitement" in keeping those rules. Bragging about that zeal may have been as much a mark in Saul's day as it is in our own.

Zeal is a hallmark of our times. Our typical conversation usually includes how hard we've been working (or how much), how much fun we've had (or hope to have soon, when we don't have to work so much), or how much we lament our work or lack of fun. In any case, passion and drive dominate our thoughts, and maybe *that* is how something so pure and wonderful can end in tragedy: it takes over as the dominant force. The zeal begins to eat us up, and burn us out. The bush burns with fire, passion and excitement, until there is nothing left to burn.

Zeal has ambition as its bedfellow. Both complement one another. Fire and desire not only rhyme—they burn! Ambition is a tough nut to crack, for we know it is vital in one form or the other for moving forward. Yet the Bible warns of it turning toward selfishness (Philippians 2:3). Anything with a warning attached should be handled carefully, but it doesn't mean it is inherently bad. Bleach serves a positive purpose, but there's a warning attached against drinking it. The fact that there is a chance that you might accidently (or purposely) drink it necessitates the legal language against such foolishness.

No one warns you to watch out for your joy, lest it hurt people. But ambition isn't joy—its bleach. It can turn toxic, and does, the moment it turns competitive. Everyone speaks of the "great" thing, and the church is no exception. We choose a "great church," with a "great pastor." The adjective insinuates competition by its very presence, for no one wants to go to the "not-so-great church," with an "okay pastor."

For Saul, he described his zeal by telling of his persecution of the church. He showed that his passion, dedication and fire for a pure version of Judaism drove him (zeal must drive; it can do no less) to work at the eradication of the cancer he saw developing. Those who accepted Jesus as Messiah were running counter to the leadership of Israel. Those leaders had seen Jesus die on a tree, the conclusion of which the Torah said, made a man "cursed of God" (Deuteronomy 21:23).

The conclusion that Jesus was Messiah, who died as the sacrifice, would signify the end to temple worship with its priests and blood sacrifices. One ending would lead to another. Jesus represented not only eternal life to those who followed Him, but the end of a way of life to an entire tribe of Israel.

If Levi is no longer the priestly tribe, what are the economic implications to a nation built on a form of theocracy? What happens to the tithe, now that there are no priests to support? What happens to the temple, the Jewish "heaven on earth" if Jesus is really "Christ in you," and the body is the "temple" of the Spirit? What about the thousands of shepherds, and the hundreds of thousands of lambs, goats, pigeons and turtledoves? What happens to the economy of sacrifice if Jesus is the once and for all sacrifice? If Jesus cleared the moneychangers from the temple when He was on the earth, what if that was to foreshadow what His death and resurrection would accomplish? The questions are endless, and Saul knew it. Holding on was more important than finding the answers.

I think many are still in the mode of zealous defense—holding on—rather than truly dealing with tough questions. There are others who use zeal to lash out—often hatefully—to defend their doctrines, ideologies and convictions. We should take time and respect the effort (why believe in something you wouldn't defend?), but let's not stop there. We can be open to a different opinion or conclusion, and we can hear it, filter it, use what is useful and discard what isn't. This isn't passivity or the acceptance of error. It's maturity.

Saul's zeal led to outright crime against the followers of Jesus. His was a drive taken to its darkest place, where zeal meets ambition gone to seed, and his measure of greatness was to use persecution as evidence that he was as driven, as passionate, and as fiery as anyone else. Let's not confuse his description as approval of zeal taken to that degree, just his usage of that zeal to show to what lengths he would go to defend the version of righteousness and religion he held most dear.

If we learn no other lesson from Saul, let's not miss this one: Zeal for God will be commended by nearly everyone, but not all zeal is fruitful and worthwhile. In his letter to the Romans, Paul acknowledged the zeal of his Jewish brethren, but said that it was "not according to knowledge" (Romans 10:2). Their ignorance led them to "seek to establish their own righteousness," and led to a failure to submit to the righteousness of God (Romans 10:3). Paul was basically describing Saul—and Paul didn't like Saul!

CONCERNING RIGHTEOUSNESS (WHAT TO EXPECT BECAUSE OF WHAT I DO)

Our previous point from Romans dovetails into this final statement by Paul. Concerning the righteousness that came by the law, Saul would have been considered blameless.

It's quite possible that we haven't fully comprehended the power that the ingrained law held in the life of the typical Jewish man in the time of Paul. The structure was deep and went much further than most of us could imagine. People today who argue whether or not we should be under the law miss a majority of the instances in which they would be in breach of Mosaic Law.

For example, while arguing in favor of law-keeping, they wear denim pants with cotton underwear. Wearing two different fabrics together was prohibited under Mosaic Law (Leviticus 19:19). This is just one example of legal infraction that we miss, but that was deeply imbedded in the average man. Saul was the shining of example of someone who did it all, and did it well.

Paul saw Saul's error, and said as much declaring that, *"Christ is the end of the law for righteousness to everyone who believes"* (Romans 10:4). You and I were never under the law anyhow, but even if we had been, it contains nothing to put us in right-standing with God.

"Concerning righteousness" speaks to the expectation we have when we do the things we think God demands of us. If we think we will be cursed when we fail, the flip side is the expectation of good as a reward for doing things right. This give and take is so common that we embrace our culture's maxims: "God helps those who help themselves," and "What comes around goes around." Saul would have embraced these, and rightfully so. Saul was under the Old Covenant.

The list presented to us most commonly in the church today includes the mandate of what we should do, now that we are saved or are part of the church. This is followed by a detailed game plan as to how to do it, and finally, the "carrot in front of the donkey," we are told what to expect if we do what we should—and what we are guaranteed if we fail.

Common sense dictates that there is no harm in letting people know what is expected of them, or to put a goal out in front of people for them to shoot for. However, if we attach our identity to what we do, then we will base our value on our ability to perform, rather than on who we are in Christ.

I think we borrowed the list from Saul, the prime example of Pharisaical obedience, religious zeal (he was "on fire for God!"), and sublime righteous standards. He was the boy you want to bring home to mother. He was the shining example of godliness. But as we are soon to find out, when Saul met Jesus, he left that identity behind. Paul had different ideas about obedience, zeal and righteousness, and he had a few choice words about the version upheld by Saul.

ENTERING REST

Paul's three–point sermon is still driving Christians to this day:

- What you should do … *(Concerning the law)*
- How you should do it … *(Concerning zeal)*
- What you can expect to get out of it … *(Concerning righteousness)*

RESTFUL SONS AND STRESSFUL SERVANTS

This list is the menu on the table in most churches: what is expected of you, the attitude we want you to take while you do what is expected of you, and if you do what is expected of you with the right attitude then here is what you ought to expect to receive in return.

We place that menu into almost every area of our Christian walk. We want to get something from God, so we determine what must be done our part, and with what appropriate level of passion and commitment. It seems only natural that if we are going to get from point A to point B we have to meet the requirements.

While effort may very well work in getting us from point A to point B in the realm of natural, day-to-day things, it is a poor substitute for the grace of God in the realm of the spirit. Whenever we start putting our hands to the process of receiving favor, anointing, blessing, etc., we do not find ourselves in the restful place of Paul, but rather in the stressful place of Saul. In that moment, we have lost our rest, forgotten our covenant, and like Samson with a shaved head and gouged eyes, we spend our time pushing and grinding another man's corn (Judges 16:21).

Samson lost his seven locks of hair (seven was a number of perfection, completion, and rest for Hebrew people, because God rested from Creation on the 7th Day). The loss of hair symbolized his loss of covenant confidence, which had been the source of his superhuman strength. His eyes were gouged out where he could not see for himself anymore, and now he had no ability to walk forward of his own volition. The loss of his liberty was equal to the loss of his rest. A captive of the Philistines, he was forced to grind the corn, so he put his head down and kept working. What else could he do? He had stepped down from a superior place to an inferior place. He had surrendered the life of a son for the life of a slave.

When we push the millstone long enough, (what to do, how to do it, and what to expect out of it), then we start to approach Christianity as a slave—forced into a set of actions and performances in order to be met with approval. We surrender the covenant rest of a son, who has the knowledge of who he is and what his father thinks of him.

Sons don't face the day in the same manner as servants. Servants awake in the morning and face a list of demands, and they work to accomplish those demands so they can be rewarded at the end of that day. Sons face the day with identity, and they work out of (not toward) that identity. They awake with the thought, "I am my father's son. Whatever he has, I have!"

Let's look again at Jesus' third story in the "Lost" trilogy. A prodigal is a "waster," and both boys in the story are guilty of as much.

The younger brother lived wildly and wasted his money. He was a prodigal with what had been given to him, and moved so far from the values of his youth that he found himself feeding an unclean, forbidden animal, and longing to eat its food! He spent his wealth and his health, and surrendered his superior position for an inferior one. His riotous living ended with the grinding of another man's corn.

The elder brother worked the fields and wasted his life. He was a prodigal with who he was, and what he could have had. He wasted years of his life, and put stress on his mind, surrendering the superior position of a son for the inferior position of a servant. His labor ended with frustration in the field, a joyless existence, and the inability to celebrate light in the dark world he had created.

Consider that last sentence. What a world some occupy: dark and dreary and hellish, with no room for joy and rest. When we live with the performance mentality—doing to get—we are going to be like the older son who stood out in the yard, refusing to party when the younger son returned home.

<u>Luke 15:25-32</u>

Now his older son was in the field. And as he came and drew near to the house, he heard music and dancing. So he called one of the servants and asked what these things meant.

And he said to him, "Your brother has come, and because he has received him safe and sound, your father has killed the fatted calf."

But he was angry and would not go in. Therefore his father came out and pleaded with him.

So he answered and said to his father, "Lo, these many years I have been serving you; I never transgressed your commandment at any time; and yet you never gave me a young goat, that I might make merry with my friends. But as soon as this son of yours came, who has devoured your livelihood with harlots, you killed the fatted calf for him."

And he said to him, "Son, you are always with me, and all that I have is yours. It was right that we should make merry and be glad, for your brother was dead and is alive again, and was lost and is found."

The older son was angry. "I haven't been given what's mine! How much do I have to work to get anything out of this? What do I have to do? How much more zeal do I have to show? I've walked the steps, and I did it with passion—here's what I expect!"

His performance had mentally divorced him from both his father and his brother. Notice, he didn't say, "My brother has come home," but rather, "This son of yours." For the older son, the separation from the family is complete.

Ambition has also created a competitive rift for the brother. It hasn't been enough to be the oldest brother—he has needed to be the best son. This is Cain and Abel reimagined in the New Testament. When I read this story, I can't help but wonder, "Why the competition?" The separation experienced by the older brother was of his own doing, and it was all in his head!

Paul said as much to the Colossians:

Colossians 1:21
> *And you, who once were alienated and enemies **in your mind** by wicked works, yet now He has reconciled ...*

The "work" the older son was doing for his father was probably "right" by all accounts, but it had become wicked, as it mentally separated him from the right to call himself a son. The work was also rooted in an effort to become something, rather than a work out of identity. Work from identity is beautiful, and we were created for such (Ephesians 2:10), but work to establish identity is wicked, and spawns an illusion of separation.

Dad responds, "Son, you and I have always been together and whatever belongs to me, belongs to you! Throwing a party for your brother is the right thing to do because he had died to us, but he is now alive again."

What theology! We live in the Father's house, and what is His, is ours. We can celebrate radical, irrational, illogical grace as we watch people go from being dead in their understanding of God and His love, to alive in the knowledge of who they are in Christ. The church shouldn't run from the message of God's grace—they should run to it, and abandon all others.

For so long, so many of us thought that a lack of receiving from God was a reflection on our poor performance for God. In reality, we do not lack because we do not work. We have not because we do not ask (James 4:2-3). Remember the words of the Father to the elder brother, and know they are the same words to you: "Son, you and I have always been together, and everything I have belongs to you."

RAIN DANCING

It seems to me that one the most damaging things that can happen to a child of God is to perceive a move of the Spirit as a reward for their actions in the flesh. In other words: do a bunch of stuff, grind the corn, and then "God moves."

When that happens, we often think God moved as a *result* of our actions. Then, as experience has taught me, we duplicate the action, expecting that at the next meeting, or service, or opportunity, we will get the same movement, or emotion, as we had before.

What happens when we don't get the spiritual response or reward that we anticipated? We pick up the stressful Saul mentality, and go through the checklist of do's and don'ts, rights and wrongs, adding to and taking away in an endless attempt to satisfy God.

I liken this to rain dancing—a form of spiritual witchcraft at work in the church. It is the belief that if we dance long enough, it will rain. The truth seems fairly simple: it will eventually rain. If you dance long enough, it will rain. If you don't dance at all, it will rain. The difference is that when we dance, and then it rains, the connection is just too hard for us to resist.

While logically elementary, the dangerous bi-product of our belief that our dance had something to do with the rain is that we focus all of our attention on the dance, rather than the enjoyment of the rain. We are often not many steps away from the start of the First Church of the Dance, complete with fund-raising machinery, by-laws and rules, and topped off with a couple bestsellers on how to guarantee rain in your area.

Don't forget the message of Paul (a message he no doubt would have preached to his former self, Saul), that the one who does miracles in your midst does not do them by the works of the flesh, but by the hearing of faith (Galatians 3:5).

One person, believing and receiving a move of the Spirit, is enough to shake the house. One other person, who is blessed to be there, but has worked their spiritual fingers to the bone all week to see a move of God, may naturally misinterpret the falling of the rain as a result of their week-long dance. The rain falls on the just and the unjust alike—and it falls on those who have been believing and those who have been working. Who is to say that the guy doing all the work isn't the reason for the blessing?

Jesus' story of the Prodigal answers that question. The Father was not good because the older brother was good. The Father was good, and the older brother, (with all of his idiosyncrasies and his hatred) could have had any and all of it at any time!

Do you want to go in to the party you don't deserve, thrown by a Father who irrationally loves you? Or do you want work one more field, and wonder when the Father will kill a fatted calf for you?

Chapter Four

JESUS CHANGED EVERYTHING

If ambition is a tough nut to crack, as we stated in a previous chapter, then Saul was the toughest nut of all. The life of high performance had given him a thick skin of confident self-righteousness. Not even the powerful preaching and impassioned plea of Stephen the Evangelist had any effect on Saul.

It took a personal revelation.

Saul probably felt good about himself as Stephen was stoned to death. Stephen's execution was confirmation that Saul was doing the right thing—defending pure religion. Once Saul had become Paul, the stoning of Stephen surely haunted him, as he faced his own persecutors and accusers. Perhaps the actions of Saul helped shape those of Apostle Paul. The site of Stephen lying in the road was probably always in the back of his mind, and could have made facing his accusers cathartic for Paul. It gave him a chance to atone for Saul. Though Jesus is our atonement, remembering our Saul can be useful in shaping our Paul.

I don't believe a revelation that transforms your mind, your heart and ultimately, your doctrine, happens because you found the right preacher, nor does it happen because you found the right church. I believe it happens when we've become so exhausted with being Saul that there's nothing left to do except quit, or become Paul.

People ask me all the time, "How are we going to get our friends and our neighbors into a revelation of grace?" My answer is to let a drowning man get to his last breath. If you jump into the water too soon, he's only going to try to drag down the both of you. Remind them often of who they were saved to be: sons of God. As they grind the corn to their exhaustion, perhaps their hair will grow, and they will remember what they have forgotten—they came into this to join Father's family, not His work force.

If you force the issue with people who aren't ready, you will find yourself in a theological argument with people who use Scripture to defend bondage, and they will exhaust you. They will always find another verse to use out-of-context—away from the finished work. There are plenty of verses in the Old Testament and the Gospels, pre-cross, that you can use for an argument if you want to ignore the finished work as a doctrine.

I'll not endeavor to equip you with rebuttal verses, but I would challenge you to take a moment and consider the impact of the following:

<u>Hebrews 8:13</u>
In that He says, "A new covenant," He has made the first obsolete. Now what is becoming obsolete and growing old is ready to vanish away.

We are confronted with a new covenant, contrasted with an old or "first" covenant. Hebrews tells us that the first is "obsolete," and at the time of the writing, it was "growing old," and was "ready to vanish away."

I'm not sure we can be fair to the authority and power of the New Covenant if we continue to prop up the verses that highlight the glories of the Old Covenant with the same validity, efficacy, and power as we do those that speak of the finished work of the New Covenant. Sure, we could produce a lot of verses to defend bondage, but when we start to filter things through a revelation of Jesus, and what He has done for us, it is time to turn the page on Saul, and move on to Paul.

LOST AND FOUND

Philippians 3:7
But what things were gain to me, these I have counted loss for Christ.

This is beautiful. Savor it for a moment. All that Saul considered profitable, and worthy of praise, Paul was willing to sacrifice at the altar of Christ. He did not see them as a "learning experience," (though learning from them is probably a good idea) or an opportunity for growth (though if you are going to have a past, you might want to grow from it). Paul was starker than we might be. For him, what he had gained in Saul was simply time lost on the planet.

When I came into the revelation of grace, I went through some bitterness. I lost those years that I could have been free—while I was grinding another man's corn, often helping with someone else's destiny. All the while I was building another man's dream, I could have been at liberty and I wasn't.

I had to be healed of that bitterness and released from its grip. It entrenched itself in my mind and snuck out in my preaching and teaching. I had to deconstruct, and learn how to construct without staying in demolition mode. It took a while, and honestly, there are still some moments when I realize there is more healing to be done. Turning my sledgehammer into a framing hammer has been my own "swords to plowshares" experience.

My revelations now are less about a change in theology (though theological changes seem to be ongoing to the point that I wonder, "Will it ever stop?"), and more about the type of grave clothes that are still being stripped away from me—releasing me into the glorious liberty of understanding that I am better as a son than as a servant. I think you will find a better version of yourself as well if your identity is found in knowing your Father, rather than working for him.

I've tried to move away from titles and acknowledgments because I began taking so much pride in them, and based my confidence in what that title represented. It can be like a drug to hear, "This is Pastor … This is who he is … this is what he does." I have come to realize that in a lot of ways, I simply lost time at being an untitled son while I worked so hard at being a titled servant.

Philippians 3:7-8
But what things were gain to me, these I have counted loss for Christ. Yet indeed I also count all things loss for the excellence of the knowledge of Christ Jesus my Lord, for whom I have suffered the loss of all things, and count them as rubbish, that I may gain Christ …

The translators sanitized this passage a bit too much. It has lost its edge; its punch. The King James Version has *rubbish* translated as *dung,* which is a little better, but it still lacks Paul's gusto. Paul writes here as a man with a bit of a temper, who has been hanging out with the common–folk and the street people. He digs into their language and their culture, and uses a word that would be a bit too offensive for many if we were to print it in a book based around theology. Use your imagine. It isn't dung, but it sure smells like it!

For Paul, all that he had held so dear as Saul stunk to high heaven. He found nothing to be impressed with in the pomp and circumstance of Saul's religion. The actions, which had brought Saul so much pride and favor among men, Paul considered to be worthless in the grand scheme of things. The glory of the day in the life of the servant holds less splendor than the darkest night in the life of the son.

Philippians 3:9
> *... that I may gain Christ and be found in Him, not having my own righteousness, which is from the law, but that which is through faith in*

Christ, the righteousness which is from God by faith.

How are we found in Christ?

When people see us there, do they see our self-righteousness? Are we closely identified with Saul, living out our lists of "What I Do," "How I Do It," and "What I Expect?" Paul was determined—and I think we should be as well—to find his identity in Christ rather than in his own ability and performance.

Saul has to go—that guy is not found in Christ. That guy is found in his works, and that is why he is eventually burned out, and ready for an encounter. His failure to perform and live up to righteous standards is inevitable, as is the crash–and–burn condemnation that accompanies that failure. If you are going to be found in Christ, you cannot have your own law–based, obedience–based righteousness. Instead, have the righteousness, which is from God through faith in Christ.

Chapter Five

DEAD AND ALIVE

RESURRECTION FROM THE DEAD

<u>Philippians 3:10-11</u>
That I may know Him and the power of His resurrection, and the fellowship of His sufferings, being conformed to His death, if, by any means, I may attain to the resurrection from the dead.

When I was first introduced to the finished work of Christ, and the revelation of what Jesus accomplished began to take root, it set me on a life–changing journey. All I had known of the finished work of Christ was the belief that in order to enact that finished work, I needed to die a little more every day.

This led to my morning ritual of praying, "Lord, I realize that it's all been accomplished in the finished work of Jesus, and so I pray that you help me to die today so that I can live for Jesus." From there, the day consisted of me hoping to be a little less at the end of the day than I was at the beginning.

As you can imagine, this formed within me a "Christianity of death," void of resurrection life. It seemed there was always something inside of me, manifesting through my actions, that needed to be killed—thus the daily return to the cross. I could never really get over it, therefore I could never truly resurrect.

In this theology, there is little emphasis on the resurrection, as it is subservient to the cross. It was the cross—the death—that took center stage. The resurrection seemed to exist simply as proof that death didn't win in its battle with Jesus.

Doctrinally speaking, the resurrection was a separate revelation that one could have only when they had sufficiently and properly died at the cross. Since I kept messing up, obviously I wasn't learning the lesson of Calvary. Therefore I wasn't ready for the lesson of the empty tomb.

This is a trap. Can you see it? Any mistake means you have yet to die on the cross, spiritually speaking. Without the cross, how could you resurrect? Simply, you can't! Therefore, you are always dying and never really living.

Please don't get me wrong, I completely understand the necessity of preaching the finished work of Jesus at His cross, but if we always point out failure, we make it appear as if the cross exists as Christ's death exclusively, rather than as our own. Paul concluded that, *"If One died for all, then all died"* (2 Corinthians 5:14). By concentrating people on the constant need for death, we leave them no hope for moving forward and learning the glorious privilege that is ours, to *"love life and see good days"* (1 Peter 3:10).

The message that is birthed from the "die to self" doctrine sounds something like, "If you have an issue, it is because you have not died yet," or "You have an issue because you haven't yielded that area to the cross … So, go get crucified!"

How do you do that?

The problem is that nobody can really describe what it means to go to the cross and die. We know we don't physically do it, because how would that help? Actually dying is certainly a way to get over your issue, but it's not a very efficient one! Do we simply pray? How do we know if we have done it correctly?

The most common answer leaves little hope: If you fail, you know you haven't submitted to the cross. In other words, you never really know until your next failure, and then you know for sure. Surely, Christ died and rose again for more than this.

I both participated in, and conducted, many altar services with Christians coming forward, crying and begging God to kill stuff in them, or take it away from them. "Take this issue away from me. Take the slavery of this issue away from me ... set me free from this. I want to die to this! How do I die to this?" This is why the church world I was attached to became all about dying. The message was always about sacrifice—lay yourself out before the Lord and pray, "Kill this in me ... crucify this in me ... I die to this ... I die to self."

Not coincidently, where this is the doctrinal focus, the outlook on the world at large is usually bleak, bordering on hateful, and the church generally focuses more on the after–life than their actual life, longing for a grand exit from the planet.

Consider Paul's argument about the death of Christ: *"I am conformed to His death."* The import of this cannot be overstated, and it will not be the token time that Paul presents it.

CONFRONTING PERFORMANCE

There were many churches in Galatia scattered throughout the region, most of which Paul had helped to establish. He founded them on the preaching of the pure grace of Christ.

After hearing that many agitators had snuck in among the ranks, and were presenting a form of gospel that mixed performance with the finished work of Christ, Paul took up his pen and wrote the letter we know as the book of Galatians.

Galatians 1:6-7

I marvel that you are turning away so soon from Him who called you in the grace of Christ, to a different gospel, which is not another; but there are some who trouble you and want to pervert the gospel of Christ.

Paul took a hard stand in defense of the gospel of grace, going so far as to confront Peter, and rebuke him to his face for what Paul considered hypocrisy. The pressure to present a version of the gospel that would be acceptable to the Jewish leaders in Jerusalem—one in which the converts to Christ also converted to the Mosaic Law—must have been overwhelming.

Then, as now, the appeal of a works-oriented message was too much for some to divorce themselves from. Paul lost one of his own ministry team—Barnabas left him and went after Peter—because there was an attraction to this external kind of holiness.

In his letter to the Galatian churches, Paul laid out a superb argument for justification by faith theology, equaled only by his letter to the Romans. Near the end of chapter two, Paul was confronting Peter and trying to prove his case to the churches of Galatia, when he hit the peak of the argument.

<u>Galatians 2:20-21</u>
I have been crucified with Christ; it is no longer I who live, but Christ lives in me; and the life which I now live in the flesh I live by faith in the Son of God, who loved me and gave Himself for me. I do not set aside the grace of God; for if righteousness comes through the law, then Christ died in vain.

Note Paul's declaration at the beginning of the verse: *"I have been crucified with Christ ..."* In Paul's theology, that crucifixion is in his past. It is a done deal.

PERFECTLY FINISHED

As we mentioned before, the language of the New Testament is Greek, which was also the common and most universally accepted written language of the world at large. Aside from the ancient Greeks (the conquests of Alexander the Great, specifically), you can thank the Roman Empire for such a wide footprint that allowed one language to be so popular.

Jesus came on the scene at the perfect time in history. Not only was he born under the law so that He could deliver all who were under the law, He came into a world in which his Jewish brethren were scattered (like sheep without a shepherd). The Roman Empire had not only unified the written language, but they had even introduced a new method of execution called crucifixion, which would serve as a prophetic fulfillment (Deuteronomy 21:23).

The writers of the New Testament wrote in Greek, though their native tongue was most likely Hebrew. The Greek language was so commonly accepted as THE literary form that several generations earlier, a group of seventy scholars had translated the Old Testament from Hebrew to Greek—a translation known as *the Septuagint*. Based upon how much vitriol and strife accompany modern biblical translations within the church now, I can only imagine the heated discussions that happened at the Jewish dinner table over such a *secular* translation of the sacred text.

I mention this so that we understand that when the New Testament writers quote verses found in the Old

Testament, they often read differently than they did in our Old Testament. This is not because they were changing it, or because they were just guessing—it was because they were reading out of Greek, and many of our Bibles translated the Old Testament from Hebrew.

Confused yet? I hope not. Let's keep it simple. The New Testament is written in Greek, but a word-for-word translation from any language to another language is problematic. In fact, in many cases, it's simply impossible to take one Greek word and give only one English word to convey the same thought. Part of this is due to various translation issues, one of which is the most important issue of all.

The Greek language is written and expressed using different tense. A word used in Greek may appear in one tense in one place, and a different tense elsewhere, giving us a different understanding of what the author was trying to convey by using that specific word in that specific manner.

For instance, the phrase, *"I have been crucified with Christ ..."* in Greek is written in the **perfect tense**. This one is difficult even for English grammar students to grasp. We are most familiar with past, present, or future tense. Think of perfect tense this way: it describes something that happened in the past that has a relationship with the present. Example: "I have done my homework" = I finished my homework in the past. *When* the homework was finished is of less important than the fact that the **homework is finished**. Having been finished, it remains done. Short of the dog eating it, the homework cannot go back to an unfinished state.

Think of Greek perfect tense as a word or phrase in which whatever is conveyed (in this case "crucified"), happened in the past with present, ongoing, and forever results—an action has been completed and the results of the action are continuing on, in full effect.

Perhaps the New Testament's best (and easiest) example of perfect tense happens at the cross. Jesus said, *"It is finished"* (John 19:30). Remember our homework example and apply that principle here. It is presented to us in Greek perfect tense, indicating, "I finished it today, it will remain finished tomorrow, and it will continue to be finished forever." That's perfect tense.

When Paul said, *"I have been crucified with Christ,"* he doesn't put it in past tense, pointing only to his conversion on the road to Damascus. That tense might read, "I was crucified with Christ." Instead, he writes it in perfect tense, to indicate his understanding that he was crucified with Christ; he remains crucified with Christ; he will forever be, crucified with Christ.

As you can see, the message, "Go get crucified ... die to self," ignores Paul's great declaration, "I have been crucified." It's easy to see why we missed it (and messed it up!); we simply didn't understand the tense. When we understand why Paul used the word in the specific manner that he did, we also understand that we need not repeat an action that has already been done!

TAKE UP YOUR CROSS

Luke 9:23
> *Then He said to them all, "If anyone desires to come after Me, let him deny himself, and take up his cross daily, and follow Me."*

I misapplied this instruction by Jesus for quite some time. It seemed to me that He was telling me to be crucified over and over again. Otherwise, why would He use the word "daily," (a word that doesn't appear in the Matthew text of the same statement)?

Without the proper, contextual understanding of Galatians 2:20 as we discussed in previous paragraphs, it was hard for me to see it any other way. What I missed within the context was the audience to whom He was speaking, and what this instruction must have meant to them.

Jesus warned His disciples that the price of following Him would be less emphasis on their own desires, and the heightened possibility that they would die in the attempt. For them, the cross was not a symbol of victory (yet!), but one of brutal execution at the hands of the Empire.

He further assured them that some would not die until they saw Him coming in glory, meaning that they would escape the martyr's death. The *daily* risk, was the price of following Jesus.

Paul used the same idea in 1 Corinthians 15:31 when he claimed to "die daily." Read that passage and its surrounding context, and you will find that Paul isn't claiming a daily spiritual death, or a "death to self," but rather he is commenting on the very real physical threats that come his way daily. He even names the location of some of those threats, mentioning "beasts of Ephesus." The threat of Saul's old, religious friends toward Paul's new theology was daily and it was real.

Jesus made the "daily cross" statement to His disciples, in their timeline, about relevant persecution they were going to experience. He was not warning me to take up my cross in spiritual death, though surely there is some utility in the "daily cross" concept for those who desire to follow Him. We too can heed the warning that following Jesus will be costly, and that there will be death to some of our old concepts and ideologies. In this sense, the statement of Jesus is alive and well, but that is a secondary application of the passage, and knowing the difference in what Jesus was saying to them, and what He might be saying to us, is crucial.

I now see this verse as a compliment to Paul's statement, "I am crucified with Christ." Take up that knowledge, and carry it, every day. When you know you have been crucified with Him, you deny the old Adam a foothold in your life, and following Jesus becomes a resurrection experience, rather than a constant duel with death.

NEWNESS OF LIFE

Paul declared that those who were baptized into Christ were actually baptized into His death. This makes the cross of Christ, our cross as well. When He died, we died. Our understanding of that is the initial step in our new creation reality.

Romans 6:3-7

Or do you not know that as many of us as were baptized into Christ Jesus were baptized into His death? Therefore we were buried with Him through baptism into death, that just as Christ was raised from the dead by the glory of the Father, even so we also should walk in newness of life.

For if we have been united together in the likeness of His death, certainly we also shall be in the likeness of His resurrection, knowing this, that our old man was crucified with Him, that the body of sin might be done away with, that we should no longer be slaves of sin. For he who has died has been freed from sin.

This is the answer to ensuring that a free people—who have a revelation of God's grace and know they are sons of God—won't run out and sin like crazy. If we release people into the knowledge that the old man is dead, and the new man is alive in Christ, there is nothing to go back to. If the resurrected reality of our newness in Christ becomes a reality, the deadness of who we used to be will hold no appeal.

Walking in victory is not a matter of checking off the performance requirements of Saul: "What am I going to do? How am I going to do it? What do I hope to get out of it?" That list may help in tackling your day, but it is useless in defeating Saul.

Walking in victory means knowing, "I am the righteousness of God in Christ. I place my faith in His finished work. I have been crucified—I am crucified, I ever will be crucified—but since I am in Him, I am alive because He is no longer dead. If He isn't dead, neither am I. If He walks as a new man on the earth, so do I!"

We should point out that due to what Christ has done on our behalf—when we accept His death as our own, and we walk into the reality of our new creation—we are not actually walking *into* victory at all, but rather, *we are living out of victory.*

We sang the song, "Victory Ahead," when I was a child in church. In Christ, we learn that it isn't "Victory Ahead," but it IS … "Victory is Mine!"

> *Romans 6:8-11*
> *Now if we died with Christ, we believe that we shall also live with Him, knowing that Christ, having been raised from the dead, dies no more. Death no longer has dominion over Him.*
>
> *For the death that He died, He died to sin once for all; but the life that He lives, He lives to God. Likewise you also, reckon yourselves to be dead indeed to sin, but alive to God in Christ Jesus our Lord.*

Jesus died once for all. He raised up once, and we have been raised up once, so that we now walk in that newness of resurrection life. Don't subject yourself back to the prison and the slavery of your own performance. You were created to be free!

If you aren't walking in the victory that is yours by right, what should you do? The tendency is to add some works to our walk in order to put forth our best effort. This is from a misguided attempt to help ourselves, for surely that will prompt God to do His part.

Nothing could be further from the truth. Notice that when Paul told the Romans that Jesus had died once for sin, he told them to *"reckon yourselves to be dead indeed to sin."* This reckoning takes place in your own mind. So, if you aren't living out of Christ's victory on your behalf, then change your mind.

I love a good song. Melody moves me, but I *really* love a good lyric. I'm beyond impressed when someone puts a line to music that speaks gospel truth, though the artist isn't trying to write a gospel song at all. The band

Sister Hazel does this powerfully in the chorus to their song, *Change Your Mind:*

> *If you want to be somebody else,*
> *If you're tired of fighting battles with yourself,*
> *If you want to be somebody else,*
> *Change your mind ...*

SONS ARE FREE

Why did Jesus set you free?

This seems like a simple question. However, many treat freedom in Christ as the obligation to serve. They seem to think they have been set free to work for God, or to be His witness, or to give Him praise. Some believe they are at liberty so they can fulfill their destiny or purpose in the earth, or to go to heaven. Respectfully, I believe these are wrong on all counts.

Galatians 5:1 (NIV)
It is for freedom that Christ has set us free. Stand firm, then, and do not let yourselves be burdened again by a yoke of slavery.

You were set free because God loves for His kids to be free. He set you free to *be* ... not to *do*. You have spent so much of your life as a *human doing*, that it is difficult to see yourself as a *human being*.

You are not alone in this conundrum. We all fall into this trap from time to time. Consider the man who retires after 40 years of success in the business world. He thought that days full of lounging and golf would be fulfilling, but having lost the identity found in what he does, he struggles with finding it in who he is. This is the equivalent to having lost purpose or meaning. If meaning is in the *doing*, then the *being* seems less important.

This is tragic! You've been set free in Christ.

We never have to worry about how the work will get done if we release people into the identity of sonship, because sons want to build the estate. Sons are proud of their kingdom. When you introduce people to their identity—of who they are and where they belong—they want to build their community. They want to make their community safe and not give it over to crime.

Even though they are not "getting paid" to do that, they will do it because it is their kingdom.

The Kingdom is not best taken care of by the servants, but by the sons. Servants clock out and go home with no thought of what they leave behind; (sounds like the attitude of many Christians in regard to the planet; clock out and let it go to hell).

You are the flock, and He provides for you. Never forget: The Kingdom doesn't belong to the shepherds. It belongs to the sheep!

> *Luke 12:32*
>   *Do not fear, little flock, for it is your Father's good pleasure to give you the kingdom.*

When people take up the mantle of ownership— "This is mine and it belongs to me"—they protect it. The Kingdom doesn't belong to anyone but the King and His kids. Slaves cannot own the Kingdom. Slaves merely work in the Kingdom.

If you are sons and daughters of the King, then the Kingdom is yours by inheritance. If you know that to be the truth, you're going to take care of the Kingdom. Why would you sin against what belongs to you? Why would you harm the inhabitants of your own kingdom? Why would you cheat them, abuse them, steal from them and lie to them? Doing these things would be like setting fire to your own house.

If we can establish identity within God's children, then the injunctions of the law—meant for our good—will seem less burdensome. We will not avoid lying, adultery, lust, and murder because we think they separate us from God, or make Him angry. We will avoid them because we take ownership within the Kingdom, and we feel responsible for the fellow members of that Kingdom. Their pain is our pain—their success, our success. To harm them would be to cut off our own arm. Identity and ownership: the twin pillars of life in the Kingdom of God.

Awake to your identity! Have you been slopping hogs? Go home. The Father will have no quarter for your speech that you desire to be a servant, but He will have robes of righteousness to cover you with, and a party thrown in your honor.

Have you been slaving away in the field? Put down your plow and go into the Father's presence. Celebrate grace with Him and all of His children. Take possession of the Kingdom you have been working so hard to get into. Drop Saul and his religious persuasions, and embrace Paul and his message of grace and peace.

BRINGING MANY SONS!

For Israel, prior to the cross, the message of servanthood was all they could really understand. Jesus told the parable of the talents to his Jewish audience, and gave the complimentary salutation *"Well done, good and faithful servant,"* to those who had done well (Matthew 25:23).

This language was necessary when speaking to the "servant" Israel. As a people, her destiny was to be the firstborn of God (Exodus 4:22), but she had long since exchanged the living water of God for broken cisterns, and had taken the form of a servant (see Jeremiah 2 for God's case against Israel, specifically, verses 13–14).

RIGHTEOUS SAUL V. RIGHTEOUS PAUL

In his death, burial, resurrection and ascension, Jesus doesn't lay down his life to create more servants. Rather, *"It was fitting for Him, for whom are all things and by whom are all things, in **bringing many sons to glory,** to make the captain of their salvation perfect through sufferings."* (Hebrews 2:10).

Christ is bringing sons, not servants!

Grace Teaches Us

<u>Galatians 2:16-17</u>
> *... knowing that a man is not justified by the works of the law but by faith in Jesus Christ, even we have believed in Christ Jesus, that we might be justified by faith in Christ and not by the works of the law; for by the works of the law no flesh shall be justified.*

> *But if, while we seek to be justified by Christ, we ourselves also are found sinners, is Christ therefore a minister of sin? Certainly not!*

Paul asked an important question about the gospel of grace: If we preach justification by faith in Christ, and we end up falling into sin, is the message wrong?

Is it ministering sin if people that hear it, end up in sin? I'm glad Paul dealt with this, for I have confronted this attitude all over the world. People say, "Told you so! You preached grace and that guy in your church committed adultery …"

My response is this: I was raised in the church, and I saw that guy commit adultery long before the revelation of grace was taught! I was raised in the "law church," and I assure you, he would have done the same thing under the law, because the law incites sin.

Romans 7:7-11

What shall we say then? Is the law sin? Certainly not! On the contrary, I would not have known sin except through the law.

For I would not have known covetousness unless the law had said, "You shall not covet." But sin, taking opportunity by the commandment, produced in me all manner of evil desire.

For apart from the law sin was dead. I was alive once without the law, but when the commandment came, sin revived and I died.

*And the commandment, which was to bring
life, I found to bring death. For sin, taking
occasion by the commandment, deceived me, and
by it killed me.*

Do you want to have a sin revival in your church?
Bring in the commandment! Paul said, "I did not know
it was covetousness or lust until someone preached to
me 'Thou shalt not covet,' and sin revived."

Rather than re-introducing people to a list of rules
and regulations, release people into liberty. Show them
that they are the righteousness of God in Christ.

2 Corinthians 5:21
*For He made Him who knew no sin to be sin
for us, that we might become the righteousness of
God in Him.*

Christ was made to be sin so that you could be made
the righteousness of God in Him. If Christ was made
sin, died, and then raised in a newness of life—likewise
we were crucified with Him, died with Him, and we
have been raised in a newness of life. We need to live
every day in this awareness.

As we stated before, there are those who are afraid that if we teach this and release people into the freedom Christ purchased, then people are going to go out and sin like crazy. They try and counter–balance grace with performance, so that grace doesn't get "out of hand." Paul disagreed that balance was needed to bring either salvation or instruction.

> <u>Titus 2:11-12</u>
> *For the grace of God that brings salvation has appeared to all men, teaching us that, denying ungodliness and worldly lusts, we should live soberly, righteously, and godly in the present age.*

Grace teaches us to deny ungodliness. When we pour in the grace of God, it teaches us that we are not who we used to be. Only grace teaches us that we are no longer righteous Saul—we are righteous Paul.

As is obvious of all sons, there is responsibility with liberty. A son with no responsibility is no less a son, though he may be less effective in ruling his Kingdom. We cannot counterbalance grace with performance, but we do need to continue to look at the performance that should be coming out of grace.

Speaking to believers as if their performance will cost them their identity is to preach an old covenant, anti–Christ message. That group will leave the church building with a "Saul" identity. Speaking to believers that their identity should produce an heir that rules the Kingdom properly, is the way to orient God's children in a world trembling for them to manifest themselves (Romans 8:19). These leave the building with a Paul identity, and a mandate to make the world around them a little less terrible.

CONCLUSION

If you've never placed your faith in Christ, I think the greatest message you could hear would be about God's people being released into freedom through a man named Jesus and the gift of His grace. The opportunity is in front of you to recognize His death as your own.

2 Corinthians 5:14-15
For the love of Christ compels us, because we judge thus: that if One died for all, then all died; and He died for all, that those who live should

live no longer for themselves, but for Him who died for them and rose again.

I make a conclusion about you today, even if you know nothing about Jesus: your death happened 2,000 years ago in a place called Calvary.

Perhaps you have never heard of the possibility of a resurrected reality. You may have been working yourself to death through your performance and your works, hoping you tip the final balance from your bad deeds to your good. Or maybe you believe in God's grace, but you view the Christian life as one of constant death and purging. In any case, I believe the perfect tense finished work of Jesus is in your past, can be yours in the present, and can assure you of eternal hope. But it really doesn't matter that I believe it for you.

One of my favorite moments in the Gospels is found in Matthew 9. A woman with a bleeding issue reached through a crowd surrounding Jesus, and touched the hem of His garment. She reached out in faith, knowing that she was ceremonially unclean and should not be touching anyone in her condition. But in her desperation, she saw hope in the man, Jesus. If He is what they say He is, then her uncleanness is not too great for His ability. She was instantly healed of the bleeding and shrank away from Jesus in awe, hoping to get lost in the crowd.

Jesus won't have it! He wants her to know that her healing was received on faith terms, and not stolen. He also wants her to go away healed, but with information.

He turns to her and says, *"Daughter, your faith has made you whole,"* (Mark 5:34). That is the first time in the Gospels that Jesus ever calls anyone "Daughter."

By addressing her as daughter, was Jesus encouraging law-breaking? I don't think so. Rather, I think it encourages us to break free from whatever law leads to death and to identify ourselves as sons and daughters of God.

If we unleash everyone into their liberty, some people are going to, admittedly, run like crazy. That is the inevitable response of newly freed people. They have been *"faking it till they make it"* for so long, that once they realize they are free to run into another yard, they are going to try to eat out of someone else's feed dish. That may happen, but don't worry about it. Release people. People will come home to where the food is.

Just like the younger son, they will come back saying, "I tried all the other junk, I have slopped the hogs, and I'm ready to come home to be a servant."

Just as Jesus would have none of the woman shrinking away, your Father will have none of your "servant" talk! He interrupts His son to declare that he is still a son, and that there is a robe, and shoes, and a ring, and food, and a party all available to him.

Also, there is no speech about the pigpen, either what happened there or threats against future hog slopping.

His acceptance of the younger son is his invitation to the older son (and to all of us): *"You are no servant here. You are still a son. Here are your shoes, your ring, and your robe. We'll kill the fatted calf to celebrate. Don't come home and serve me—come home and love me, because I've always loved you, and all that I have is yours!"*

ABOUT THE AUTHOR

Paul White is an internationally recognized author, teacher, and conference speaker. He has pastored, and taught in churches and conferences around the world in his 25+ years of ministry. Paul received a Master's Degree in Theological Studies from Regent University in Virginia Beach, Virginia.

Seeing believers experience an awakening to the goodness of God's grace through Jesus is Paul's greatest passion. He is a messenger of hope and grace for the world, removing grave clothes from God's resurrected people. He hosts a daily podcast and posts sermons and videos from around the world on his website, PaulWhiteMinistries.com. He has published two other books: *Revelation To Transformation* and *Between the Pieces.*

Paul and his wife NaTasha have two children: Lukas and Lauren. They currently host a weekly meeting and base their ministry operations in beautiful Flowery Branch, Georgia, while traveling to share the good news with people around the globe.

RESOURCES

Between The Pieces:

What Really Happened At The Cross

> This book takes the reader behind the scenes at the cross, past the physical death of Jesus and on to a remarkable glimpse into the spirit realm. At Calvary, there were prophecies fulfilled, promises made and possibilities opened to the entire world. Go between the pieces to find that when Jesus died, His death was more than just the sacrifice for sin. At the cross there was a covenant confirmed, a covenant fulfilled, a covenant broken and a brand New Covenant provided.

Revelation to Transformation:

How Seeing Jesus Will Change Your Life

> Most of us have become accustomed to the constant preaching and teaching of guilt and condemnation. This slowly but surely pulls our eyes off of the loveliness of the finished work and onto the unfinished areas of our lives. Our problem is not the absence of knowledge that we need help. Rather, it is the utter inability to help ourselves. In this book, the author explores how Calvary was God's intervention in all of our issues, and how Jesus has delivered us from fear of eternal punishment by being punished in our place!

Order Online at www.PWM-store.com

Made in the USA
Columbia, SC
24 November 2018